HIGH BLOOD/PRESSURE

HIGH BLOOD/PRESSURE

by
Michèlle T. Clinton

West End Press

Grateful acknowledgment is made to the publications and recordings where some of these poems have previously appeared: *Alcatraz, Barney, Electrum, Insurgence, Issue One, Juke Box Terrorists with Typewriters, Southern California Anthology, Poetry Loves Poetry, Los Angeles Weekly, Magazine, Roh wedder, Sing Heavenly Muse!* and Freeways Records *English As A Second Language* and *Neighborhood Rhythms.*

First edition – September, 1986
ISBN 0-931122-41-4

This project is partially supported by a grant from the California Arts Council, a State Agency.

West End Press, P.O. Box 291477, Los Angeles, CA 90029.

TABLE OF CONTENTS

With deep appreciation for the criticism & encouragement
I found at the Beyond Baroque Literary Foundation poetry
workshop, I wanna thank 'specially:
Jack Skelley (& all members of the international
thrill-seeking hang),
Bob Flanagan,
Kyle Norwood,
& Nancy Hall.

And Matthew.

A FOREWORD:
On Brothers & Nigguhs

> "To admit suffering is to begin the creation of freedom."
> —Robin Morgan, *Monster*

I hope you'll be moved by these poems. Though I mean to
make my work challenging, there are two areas in which I hope I
will not be misunderstood. In exposing the violence of black men
towards black women, I do not mean to contribute to the racist myth
that black men are predisposed to violence. In fact, black men are
the victims & carriers of the diseases of patriarchy & it is patriarchy
which creates violence against women. Instead, I try to facilitate
the healing generated by the expression of experience. I work to
expose the sensitivity of the psyche & the pathology that follows
abuse. We can heal our pain, but only if we first give voice to the
depth of our suffering.

I write about black people with two contrasting words: nigger
& nigguh; nigger being that ugly insult used by hateful bigots
& nigguh being the word that black people use to talk with & about
ourselves with humor & an ironic sense of our history. With beauty
& rhythm black people have reclaimed & recreated our language:
with it we love ourselves. To our language, our survival & our
future, I offer you my work.

Michèlle T. Clinton
June 5, 1986

I WANNA BE BLACK

It was a time, that summer '66
when it always be some brother on the corner
in a beret, a leather jacket, green army pants,
wantin' to know what was a young child like me
doin' out in the night,
didn't I know it was dangerous,
why, what would your momma say?

Before the red devils & bennies
I got ten for a dollar, before
I turned to Smokey Robinson & ripple wine,
or gettin' finger fucked in some garage
by some body with a dick,

all that summer, at night time walkin',
I got schooled by miscellaneous black nigguhs
gone caring & literate
breakin' down the community party line:

Nigguhs need to pick themselves up out the drug scum,
the numb come, up out the sphere of the white man's
life plan & history & logic & systematic self hate
for black & funk & nap & snap & pop & fuck & fun
& just 'bout most the best thangs folks love to do.

And these brothers,
these big brothers would walk me home
no matter how far, how late,
& wouldn't put they hands on me
& wasn't disrespectful no kinda way.

Then my titties started growin' & I realized
I could leave my glasses home: just squint.
& then it be just 'bout guaranteed
some fool would take me by the wrist
& lead me through the shifting dance floor
at fremont high saturday night sock hop,
& grind all 'tween my thighs a full three minutes
'cause I was starting to get cute.

For a while I got so preoccupied
I guess I didn't read no books,
& after the Hampton thang
I guess other black folks
didn't wanna read no more books neither
'cause all that politicizin'
was turning out to be dangerous
to the conscientious individuals of the race
(nigguhs gettin' shot up by the FBI & carryin' on).

Or maybe we just came to a time in history
when pussy was just plain better
or maybe wine was not sour
or the devils in dope smoother
I don't know
but seemed like everybody flaked at once.

Now folks don't know who's Ron Karenga
Fonya Davis, & if you say black panther
they think you mean animal
& all the negros in dreads & greens & reds,
all the socialistic lesbian colored girls,
they so far away from this gerry curl,
this wild dancing pussy,
LA's Prince obsession & South African gold
strung 'round black necks,

it don't seem like it ever was
a functioning community,
don't seem like it coulda been more than a myth,
a wish, a desperate hallucination,
that black people could love each other
in the cool & dark of Watts America
1966.

DID SHE BLEED?

Cercie was a man built like an ape, and despite all my
consciousness about comparing a black man to an ape, my
mind still says ape when I think of him.   Ape.   Or bull.
Big ugly black bull, his barrel chest, and shining black
arms, the strong dead fat thick across his stomach.

There was food then.   Always meat & regular meals.
Instead of the ice box light shining unimpeded & mustard
sandwiches & water & potatoes & potatoes & potatoes, I washed dishes,
opened the refrigerator door over & over & stared at the
neck bones, the leftover greens & yellow corn bread.

At first the nights were quiet.   The breaths of my
mother's bed.   They whispered.   But then she talked
faster, and Cercie commanded, she talked faster in
short jabs, then loud, loud through the night came
her groan, all raspy, like she was throwing up.
Then silence.   The bed creaked.

All was terror in our house, with meals
& cleanliness, that terror.   That she could not tell him
to go, because of meat & bottles & pleasure, he could
be here & do whatever he wanted & she could not tell him
just go
leave
leave me & my children, go
or he would kick her.   In the ribs, I saw his foot, it
went in her side & blood came from her mouth.   Get out
my muther fuckin' house, she had yelled & in one stroke
of his thick black hand, she was on the floor & his
foot was in her ribs.

Fridays were the days, Payday.   The men & women would
come over & watch us dance & give us quarters & then
go get a bottle.   Beer was usual, she could afford
beer on her own, but Cercie bought a bottle every
Friday & then kicked her ass.   Thursdays were numb days,
the day after her bruises were gone, the day before

3

the Terror, & Saturdays were the days when the sun
shone the sharpest in the projects & folks watched
cartoons & Shirley Temple movies to keep their eyes
off the sun.   I stayed in bed as long as I could,
repelled by the broken glass, the blood & swelling
of my mother's face.   He'd be gone & she, up earliest,
would finish off the bottles, empty the warm beer cans,
the saliva dripping from her mouth.   'Look what you
let him do to me.   Look what he did.'

Negros in the Pueblos were used to it.   'OOOO, Pooki's
daddy just beat Pooki's momma's butt.'   'The police was
at Dwight's house last night.   I wonder if his momma
got a whuppin.' '   Everybody was used to it, & the purple
faced women went shopping so you saw them in the stores,
& they did their laundry so they were in the washhouse
too, everywhere swollen women & children talking fast:

Did yo' momma get whupped last night, is she missing
teeth?   Did you rush up his back, your brothers & sisters,
were you flung across the room when he stood up & flexed
his muscles?   Did you see him turn, again, to her?   Did
you hold scissors as Tarzan flashed on teevee, & twist the
blade over & over in the sun, did you cook, wash dishes,
glad for the grits to fill the hole in your stomach?

Did your momma get beat last night?
Did she bleed?

Do you remember?

4

EVICTION

White men handed papers to my mother
through a cracked door.   We had to
get boxes from the liquor store
& watch her get drunk.

Before, just yesterday, my mother
brought home purple heart doilies
& gave us large silver coins
we held tight in our hands
running to catch ice cream bells.

Yesterday she baked macaroons,
she talked to her plants & scrubbed
even the air with her sure, careful
movements.   Now she sits.   She stares;
she drinks.

And after our disassembled home,
rum, gin, & vodka boxes are carried .
on the backs of large & small men
swarming about my mother's drunken laughter,

After the doilies have been gathered,
the plants limp with root shock
are placed on the orange U-Haul,

We will jump on beds &
throw kung fu kicks at the walls,
We will break windows & shriek
as they shatter, for the unyielding blue eyes,
the unknown, untouchable Authority
that disrupted
this, the peace
of my mother's home.

AIN'T 'BOUT NOTHIN' BUT SOME TOAST

How you like yo toast be a very important thang
'cause you the only one can get toast right.

You take like eggs, 'n you say I like my eggs fluffy,
I like my eggs wit pepper, 'n if you could fry them in margarine
'stead of oil, I would like that.
'N somebody brang you eggs 'sactly like that.

But toast, no matter how good you 'splain it,
somebody brang you toast it be half way cold
or the wrong kinda bread or soggy or too brown
or sumthin' 'n it jess don' be right.

Yo momma cain't do it.   Yo runnin' partner
on mushrooms & motorcycle cain't do it,
yo second best lover wit serious head
cain't do it like you needs to get it done

when you come home, last unemployment check in hand,
nobody at the pad, bird sleepin', kitchen cold & black,
tight money funk fillin' yo mind, when caught 'tween
the rush & crash of hellacious party in the streets,
yo main squeeze don' get it up regular no more
'n you cain't stop puttin' things in yo mouth:

Time for toast, however you like it
'cause you the only one know the ins & outs
of yo tastebuds & fingertips.

Eatin' toast remind me a' flyin' a flag you don' wanna spit on,
eatin' toast remind me a' basketball, African bonding,
& dialectic materialism.   Eatin' toast say Keep hangin'
girl, the wicked system out in the streets
can fuck wit yo pocket, you nigguhs
but who got yo self
when the kitchen all cold & black,
cat snorin', roommate out chasin' pussy somewhere,
jess gimme me some Wonder bread 'n I'll be cool,

6

gimme three cigarettes, jet fuel coffee finna perk,
& steam risin' offa my hot buttered toast.

MIGRATION OF THE RATS

I remember getting dog bit,
books & teachers had said 24 hours would do it,
I'd be foaming at the mouth
& dying mad, so I tole my momma
& she said 'Let's wait & see what happens'
& I brooded how stupid that bitch was,
I could be dying
not that she was tired,
or didn't have no money for the doctors,
no ride to the hospital
'cause medical don't pay for false teeth or glasses
or dog bit treatment so we did without those things.

I read in books about the rats in Harlem,
they bit babies not 'cause rats was mean,
which they is, but 'cause rats was hungry.
In the Pueblos we didn't have no hungry rats,
just a rabid mutt without a chain
got my leg, in the projects
I never even seen a rat,
'cept when Dwight, nappy headed lil' boy
lived by the wood yard, tole me a bigger rat tale
everyday, in the units closer to the lumber yard,
he said, the rats was comin' one & two at a time,
Dwight wit his big lumpy head
got him a dead wood rat, tied it to our door knob
so I seen my first & last dead rat,
a swinging hairy thing hung by the tail on the door.
The rats was comin',
I was the smallest person in the house
& if they was gonna chew on a baby,
they'd probably chew on me
& my momma wouldn't get me to the hospital,
too tired from nuthin', or too drunk,
we'd watch the bubonic plague turn me ashy
waiting to see.

So when I do the weekend chill out
with white middle management,
if I say I'm from Watts
even the men get quiet,
'cause they know what I am then,
refuge nigger, possibly brutalized,
now quieted & relieved for the view their company affords.

But when kind women trap me with soft voices
swirling crystal glasses of juice & champagne
one on one they say
how did you make it out
like I was a university or est graduate
with cause & effect explanations for everything
& I wisht I had that rat,
wanna slap it on the ice sculpture,
wisht I had a knife of political metaphysics
to cut their vision outta me,
I wanna be a black nigguh, the dirty kind,
a skin head punk into anal sex & hard drugs,
gimme the spirit of a tired black mammy,
sour as their porcelain toilets
filled with their carnivorous farts,
lemme spit rat poison on their clean faces

'cause I didn't get outta nuthin'
'cept fear of dying
which I'm still scared of,
which the wine & pate & wit can't stop me
dreaming rat dreams,
the nightmares come even in suburbia
after rows of peaches & sliced shrimp quiche
neat in prettily arranged kitchens
of the rising, resting middle class.

"I CAN MAKE YOU FEEL GOOD"

LOVE, like LOVE, like the LOVE of a story,
the LOVE in a book
I could trust more
than a buncha nigguhs,
LOVE like a 45, Smokey Robinson crooning
his stomped heart out, I learned to cry
watching my momma listen to am radio.
In the streets, at the parties we fled
the home front to those black
cold adolescent nights, those LA
clear winters biting your neck,
I learned to grind, I reached into Temptations
of the music & the sway & the hard
eyes of a boy I did not know.
For LOVE, for LOVE in the flesh,
for grown hands around a tender beard,
a pussy that bleeds, inside & fully
a woman, open to swallow
this living LOVE.

We would open like a hole, to do a boy
& be a girl & flexible & rough tough &
ready for how they change, each a bum
hallucinating, sometimes a king & glowing
in a funky castle you will tidy,
his crown his queen will polish, his royal lady,
his poke-ee, his one to fuck & spew out
his anger on her face
if he wants, if we want & consent & give it up
to LOVE, if the solo in the song makes you hot,
up for drama, the ups & downs in a plot
implanted at adolescences in every body's brain.

That LOVE, LOVE clear & wanting
a body prone
to receive & give it up & make
that LOVE hold him, take
in the shape,

allow filling,
ready to receive
those dumb songs.

GHETTO DISEASE

I spent 4 & one half hours looking at the smeared
walls & heavy brown faces of County General, hussling
the first pap smear for a 19 year old rape victim:
my best friend.   I used up half a tank of low lead
driving to East LA to pick up my 6 year old nephew,
so now there are 5 people here on these 2 couches &
2 beds in this 1 room, & wit 5 folks eatin', the corn
meal canister is half empty, & ain't but 3 hot dogs left.

Somebody broke the metal hinges off the mail box &
stepped wit my disability check.   My brother came
in drunk 5 times & tole me he was gonna roll a punk,
or beat the shit out of a mesican, & while I kin
usually talk him outta snatchin' purses or knockin'
over liquor stores, about fightin' he tole me
'Don't chu worry none about me, I never get into
sumthin' I cain't handle, that's why I ain't got no
scars on my face.   'N I ain't gonna do no time
behind no punks.   The man don't care about faggots &
mesicans.   They's free game in this neighborhood.'

So when I asked my calm faced doctor what I got to
do to get well, so I kin work, buy groceries & move, he said
'Stress.   Eliminate stress from your life & you'll be fine.'

And just today I decided I won't go outside during
the day anymore 'cause my best partner got snatched &
pushed to her knees in broad day light, some funkey nigguh
tipped off with 97 dollars of my uncashed money, &
my brother ain't got but 2 joints left.

'Fire it up man,' I tole him.   'What dat doctor
want me to do?   Quit smokin'?   Eat vegetables & lean
beef?   Take walks in the afternoon?   Relax?

Shit, brother man, pass me dah joint.
I think I'm gonna be healin' for a good while.'

WARNING TO YOUNG BRIGHT SISTERS/
WHITE AM. CULTURE 101A

Once, a pre-med white boy laced his fingers into mine
& introduced me to foreign films, espresso in cafes, & existentialism.
As far away from niggerism as I could get, I ran to him,
relieved to be caught by his thighs & fucked,
dry, for hours & hours & hours.

Hardened black faces filled the ceramic cups
& picked up the tips he left.   I brooded,
& after Camus had been exhausted I suggested
Ntozake, Jean Toomer, Baraka.

"Why are you so angry?" he told me, & dropped my hand
when black men passed us on the street;
"Where do these moods come from?"

His childhood of piano lessons & little league,
an occasional bloody nose & a fat idle mother
was a calm crack in the black rat faces that haunted me
at night.   The fissure grew & grew by white magic,
white power I wanted to be swallowed & cleansed.

I told him about mine: 2 and one half rapes,
nigguhs cutting up my younger brother,
cardboard in the bottom of shoes when it rained,
& poetry books I stole from the library.
Fatigued, he poured French coffee, lit a cigarette
& picked up Sartre.   "Strive to be positive," he told me,
looking up from his book, "or at least impartial."

Impartiality scalds the tips of tongues into silence:
I said nothing.   The crude dry lessons of hot white men
can make you numb.   Or spin in anger exponential to street abuse,
or thrash in dizzy shame of black innocence.
Impartiality burns blind in young white men who feel
the hope of Nietzsche, the power of privilege
& the servitude of women who want only to escape.

MIXED HOSTILITY

My grandmomma is a white woman,
my momma mulatto,
so what does that make me?

I have smooth brown skin, & good hair,
all the women in my family have good hair,
& all the women in my family gray around 30,
& eventually bald, so good hair is a trick bag
on many levels.

My momma is mulatto.   Vanilla fudge, vanilla fudge
we say when we see the golden brown babies,
carried by them drug beaten white girls
in the Haight, wit no man at they side.
We say Vanilla fudge, vanilla fudge,
Nigguhs 'n they white girls,
nigguhs 'n they white girls.

Must confuse a nigguh pretty bad to wake up
& find they momma is white.
Yeah, they momma is a white girl, who used to be into brothers.
"Brothers."   That means yo own self Daddy,
who ain't nowhere on the set.
Must confuse a nigguh to wake up to sumthin' like that.

Then you see them same kids years later talkin' 'bout
"I just can't seem to relate to black people"
'n "Black women aren't anything particularly special to me."
So we shake our heads.
That vanilla fudge gots a hard way to go.

Momms didn't know who she was,
& still for me the enemy blurs & escapes
into brothers with blue eyes & sisters with creamy skin.

& I confuse other people:
"You mixed wit sumthin'?"
"Naw, I ain't mixed with nuthin' "

"You look like you could be mixed with Indian or sumthin' "
"Naw, I ain't mixed with shit.
It's all the way negro here."

What I'm 'posed to say now:
My grandmomma is a white girl.
I love black people
& spite white.
I have good hair
destined to thin & chalken
& my grandma, grandma is white.

INTERNATIONAL COLOREDS: SAY WHAT?

We nigros wit white kin
close as a generation away
a momma or daddy with
some bizarre social circumstance
Here we is honey colored or brown
introducing a lighter brother:
a white boy!?   We mocha mixes
got lots to say to the other
cross breeds: Mix a new york jew
wit a puerto rican from the east
bronx, & what do you got, a
people stew & cross prosperity
contradictory alliances
with the story of the color line
the racially ambiguous
who slip into other cultures
can dance salsa or reggae
will speak with a british
accent 4 minutes into London
tan in a week deep brown
& catch hell in Greece
just like regular nigguhs so.

I don't wanna be no cutie pie
fox 'cause of white feathers
& curly hairs, don't wanna get favors
special allowances
jobs in the media 'cause we ain't
as scarey as the real spooks
burly & thick tongued
the trust of the white man
manifests as money & mobility
I don't wanna feel the historic hate
well up in the eyes of black people
aimed at the white man, but it's
hitting my neck, my vagina

Don't wanna buy into it, feel into it
fall into the cross fire of homelessness
In innocent fucking lust
I got here – my people
want a silent blending
of my life into theirs &
I wanna dialogue.

ON SEX IN JULY

for Matthew

Mostly I think about protecting the slit,
about mace classes from the police
& my spiked brass knuckles
I keep by my keys,

& I think about a window that might be cracked
& the wicked men who carry the mail or bag my food
& the women who suffer sex in war
who have holes to brutalize
babies to butcher,
that special female vulnerability.

Once a month my blood is brown & thick
instead of thin & bright
'cause the best freedom from abortion is chemical
pills that swell breasts for men to suckle.

Then he that fills me with his life
comes near & spreads my lips with his fingers,
he that whimpers like a child for a tit,
for some sympathy against this harsh world,
he stiff & hard, groping for something round & soft,
while from inside
my vagina grips & sours
against its openness,
against its need
I can't feel anymore
& it's summer
so hot
the maniacs might get lonelier,
hornier, might telepathically sense my open patio,
might think to bring a screwdriver,
a loaded gun for my mouth,
an ice pick for my anus.

While he that comes to me in the night
when the blue fan hums,

18

worn sheets from his mother
strewn across the floor, he
my lover, my baby, my boy
comes with lemon & ice in sweating glasses
to cool me with electric winds
& cups of cold water,
comes to find a fleshy space of undrying promises,
& warm unspoiled giving brown soil.

FOR WOMEN WHO HATE A MAN

David has a penis he calls the Dong,
an LA Dodgers visor cap & infectious herpes.
David liked me to say 'big black dick,'
& liked me to suck it while he watched
the Disneyland Rams kick ass.

"I got some shit you ain't ready for,
I wanna do sumthin' to you you can't deal wit,"
& before that I tole him I wanted sex vanilla,
no role playin' & no extraneous equipment.
"This here's a love relationship, babe,"
I said.   Today I tell him, laughing,
"Rose chokes her man when he comes.
She chokes him, gives him red wine enemas,
& watches him stagger from the bathtub."

I wasn't strapped down but had needles taped in my arms,
& non menstrual blood on pads 'tween my legs.
Nigguh couldn't understand why I didn't wanna fuck
afterwards, besides doctor's orders & a bruised uterus.

I make him mean because of inside, that
hollow space lined with creams & blood clots,
he needs his Dong, his big black dick there, everyday,
exactly there, moving, because I have a hole
I can make him weak:

"I couldn't go with you," he tole me, "I just couldn't face it,"
so I thought I could penetrate with a broom handle.
Take a seed, a shiny black watermelon seed,
push it up his asshole & make him grow something
wretched & inappropriate
needing a good clean scrape, clinical & without sympathy.
"I got yo big black dick lover,
I got some of just what you need,
a good hard dickin' down.
This here's a love relationship,

so I want you to spread 'em,
& get ready tonight."

STAR DUST

At ten o'clock, the women come out their rooms,
their hands rubbing their thighs & backs.   They
drop coins in the pay phone & lean against the
gray wall, listening to the rings.

In my room is a color teevee, chained down,
a broken mirror, & a white lamp with a bulb
that works only when it is screwed in.
Behind yellow curtains limp & uneven,
I smoke hashish & cigarettes & wait
for the women to go away from the phone.

Though I have been known to fuck more than one man
at a time, get slapped around, free base,
& steal shiny things from middle class bathrooms,
I am a decent woman:
I don't shoot dope, never had to take a righteous
ass whuppin', & ain't never sold no pussy,
so I don't have to look at them.   I prefer
to sit behind the haze of limp curtains
& wonder at the center of the white flowers
on my broken lamp painted with red nail polish.

"Bitch.   Where my money," I hear men cursing,
"You better act right.   I ain't playin'.
Bitch, I'll stick my dick up yo ass,
I'll fuck you with my dick up yo ass hole,
I ain't playin' wit you."

My old man returns to me, his shoulders hunched
over the Times, his arms carrying white bags & brown bags.
"Look at her red pants!   I can tell she's a whore!"
"Shut up boy.   That's that scotch talking.
Can't you be polite?"
"You god damn whore!"
"Shut up man!   I got to get along wit these hoes"
"OOOO, I'm gonna fuck you tonight, baby,

I'm gonna do it to you tonight,"
as I push him through the door remembering

I am a decent woman.   I listen through
the rain to their curses, I hallucinate
unwound hangers, my man brings me wounds
wound in a taut penis, the newspaper
folded & creased, with red circles around
want ads.   We eat chicken McNuggets
with our fingers, drink Jack Daniels
from the bottle.

I am a decent woman: My old man
never has no money, so I fuck him
for free.

BLACK RAPE

I got fucked & it wasn't no thang,
just a trip 'tween a boy 'n a girl,
some pussy & cock disease
colonized our bodies,
made him take me down in an alley,
the knife still in his hand.

Just some man-woman thang,
take it like a woman,
take it like a white woman
raped by a white man,
not racially related, not culturally relevant,
take it like a woman,
bitch.

'Sides, black men are under
a lotta pressure I'm told,
got good cause to act it out.
'Sides, black boys got decent
reason to explode so

I got humped by a brother
& the sickness sucked up my cunt:
I wished for a demented caucasian,
Give me a clean hate,
I wasted a wish to make the cock white,
make the swallowing a smoother acceptable
kind of political pain.

FEMINIST MANIFESTO

No man will ever spray paint me a heart,
ask me to get hitched, meet they momma
& be that special sweet one.

Nope! For me they get the vaseline,
they buy lingerie, they make me
say over loud speakers:

I want it.   I want the drugs
between your legs.   Inject me baby.
Fuck me like I'm trash.
If you lookin' for a princess,
look someplace else.

Yes honey, I am white trash, a hungry Negress
t-totally   hip to that be bop
men usually be runnin', with them
close talks, that jewelry, them family barbecues,
have you thinkin' twice as much as you regular do
just to deal with they aunties, they potato pie,
they new songs, them fast talkin' cock slingin' boys
wanna be with you all the time
long as you goin' with them where they goin'!

I'd rather be trash! I'd rather dig deep
in a publisher's anus
wearing my rose & black G-string
hopped up on some peanut butter crank!
I'd rather watch pastel Venus star
rise alone.   I'd rather the feminist call me heifer
& my momma shake her head
than to suck the mythic bwana dick
of respectability from men.

EXECUTIONER

A broken wishbone is on our table,
& handcuffs (the police kind), old roses,
walnuts, & the usual medicinal things: cold coffee,
half a bloody mary, weed, pipe & razor.
The man comes in & yells at me:
'Where are all the chains? We don't have
enough chains in this house!' Then
he hands me black lipstick & black
nail polish: presents. 'You can use them
anytime,' I say.

'How about tonight, they'd be perfect
with these black tights, this hood.'
'You got good legs, mister man,' I say,
'You look pretty cool.' He points his toes.
'That corn flakes mirror, will you get it
for me & help me with my face? Lemme
fix you a line first.'

We always have fresh flowers: roses
that look like pussy & gardenias
that smell up the house. He rapes
the neighbor's garden for me &
always leaves at least one thorn
on each bud.

'You alright? You moving pretty slow
these days. Maybe it's your period.
You know how you get sometimes.'
'I dunno. Those counselors—'
'You called suicide prevention again?
Damn you girl, I told you you don't
have no drug problem, why you let
those people make you crazy? Here.
Take this mirror. Help me with my
toe nails. I need the black smooth.'

When he leaves, the apartment goes
blank.   When he returns he shows me
a ball separator.   'For penis torture.
I won it at the party for best dressed
executioner.'   I get him a cigarette,
a drink, & begin to fill up the pipe.
He stands up, to get matches I think,
but then he takes the cape off to show
the red welts,

the narrow swollen lines below the
nipples & across his back.   Underneath
the tights, the skin is broken: purple
spots where the blood has begun to clot.

'I played a game called Gladiator.
Three rounds against another male.'
He lifts his white head, his light
blue eyes at me & grins.   'I won,' he says,
& his hands, though not small
or scarred, are shaking.

MANIFESTING THE RUSH/HOW TO HANG

If somebody tries to give you something, let them.   This applies
to everything, especially cigarettes, sex & drugs.

Tell time to take a hike.

Laugh at everything you can.

Find people who are hanging & hang with them.   Screen them with
drugs: weed alla time, cocaine too hard on the pocket, beer'll
make you fat & gin'll make you drunk a lot quicker.   Slamming is
hard on the nerves, green pills white pills & black ones from
somebody's doctor play real well, & nobody crazy with good sense
does acid.

Tell everybody everything.   No masks, no mysteries & tell every
body you won't tell anybody, & tell anyway.

Figure out who is hanging with who.   Go to people you don't hang
with but know they hang with people you hang with, 'n say
HOW'S DAH HANG?

Establish an in clique code word for those not hanging: ya gotcha
basic square, ya gotcha pasty faced 'merican geek, bendin' over,
goin' for the okey doke.   Ya gotcha LA strangelo, ain't nan'
one of 'em know how to hang.

Open your home as a hang center.   Keep tidbits in your freezer,
stock up on ultra-stress formula vitamin B complex.   Do a lotta
dishes.   At least once a week, plan on giving over an evening to
somebody's bad trip, somebody's peel, some trim together sculptor
will do the break down & then you got to hang tough.

How to hang tough: Imagine yourself very cool,
very sharp, & altogether together.   Remember, it's fine to be
crazy, it's like really okay to be crazy, like what the fuck
else we gon' do, we got so much heart, so much insight, we livin'
in a hellacious world, man, folks like us, if we wasn't crazy,

we'd be dead or crazy, ONE! Then tell your partner. Let him know who's boss. Listen. Hold his hand. Hold him. Tell him his momma loves him. Confess something evil. Hold him. Tell him again, his momma wasn't jiving, she does love you man, she just didn't know how & it ain't nuthin' wrong wit being crazy, & you ain't crazy no way. Be prepared to knock his ass out if he gets too wild.

Regarding sexual activity, consider filthy language and lingerie. Never sleep with anybody crazier than you. Unless you go up for a wild ride. Keep your hands cupped over your heart. Do not fall in love.

TRYING TO DRAW A SQUARE POET

The hoes
call any woman
who will not turn a date
a square,
& the women
who will not turn a date
call the women
who will not shoot dope
a square,
& the women
who will not shoot dope
call the women
who will not fuck a man
they don't know just for fun
a square.
& the women who will not
fuck a man they don't know real well
just for fun, well,
who knows about them anyways.   (They squares.)

My momma is definitely
a square.   Yo momma is
definitely a square.

Nat King Cole,
suicide poems,
eating in cars,
K-Mart, handcuffs
& loud noise
could go either way,
but violence is always
cool.   (People love to
hear about violence.)

If not drugs,
weed.   If not weed,
gin.   If not gin,

Millers Light.
& if not coffee &
cigarettes,
you dealin' wit
a square.

I have a little stamp
I pass out to white folks
who show me their art work.
I say, "You cool wit me, man.
You ain't no square."
Instantly, they are relieved.

But being a square
is cool.   Some of the
coolest cool I know
is a square.
I pretend to be a square.
You pretend to be cool.
I am pretty cool about
pretending to be a square.
You are pretty god damn cool
about pretending to the square
in relation to the cool
where I am
in reality
a square.
Making all this up.
Which is: what it be like.

And definitely
pretty cool.

FOR THE KID

I am a nigger.
I am a mad nigger.
I am a mad nigguh
in love with everythang
& you are a white boy.
Just like yr bald headed faggot daddy
filled with anti-fact & anti-feeling
from yr murmuring heart & gnarly feet.

You ride a motorcycle.   You chew mushrooms.
You spit poison at the sweet women
& dare them to come near.   You hide,
you twitch, yr stomach knots.

On the other hand,
I am wild.
I ain't got no sense.
I am a wild nigguh in love with everythang
impossible, or tarnished, or dying

I put moves on short honkies with acne
& little dicks just to see them dance.
I laugh like a hanna barbera cartoon,
smile as hot & spicy as the steam
coming off a pot of Louisiana gumbo.
I know herbal remedies for hemorrhoids,
incantations for manic nightmares,
mojo, hoodoo, & little known to the
Western world nigese magic.   I raise
red angles from white ash;
I remind you to take vitamins, say grace,
& toast whenever we got alcohol.

I am a mad
        crazy
nigguh-woman.   You are a
        wicked

white
boy.

And   you   will
come
around.

GOOD PEOPLE KNOW HOW TO GREEZ

3943 Western is Red's, Redbone's,
sistah with skin as light & fresh
as lilacs & curved broad butter,
lady you know just as soon
take a sharp tongue
as a butcher knife
to anybody's behind
who step out of pocket,
girl will fix you up wit
steamin' biscuits & jelly,
brown sugar & grits,
fried eggs & porkchops
or hot links, &
jet fuel mornin' coffee
have you righteously buzzed.

So, for $3 you can
wake it up on Sunday mornings
sitting next to the
toffee stockings & powdered
faces of decent black women
coming from the A.M.E.

After eatin' like that
you got to take a shit
but see Red don't like no
white folks in her kitchen,
don't want no
stringy hairs
falling in the pancake batter,
& seein' as the bathroom
is just past the sink & grill,

If on Sunday mornin's
you white poets
grog yourself out of bed,
stretch through the hangover

& find yourself seeking
smooth coffee & ethnic
atmosphere & you got $3
& can make it over to
39th & Western,

Remember
Redbone'll fix you up good,
welcome you any place
but the toilet

so you'll have to
hold your shit
til you get back across town.

ANTI APART HATE ART

American blacks are known
for black magic & music &
humor, not black at all
but deep husky hearted
laughter that empties us
of hate.

Anti-hate we partay, we play,
make soul food easy
for white folks to swallow,
cut back on spice & the nasty
grease of history, nigguhs
be shame to be grouped
wit the jiga boos of the jungle,
beatin' drums, barefoot & ignorant.
Africa don't got the style
of new wave slick purple
pompadors, liberated negros
set the pace
in athletics, we the fastest,
hippest thang goin', doing the
well paid work of soothin' honkies
& stayin' high, hittin' the joint
to hide a shit colored memory of being
scum in this country, in this
world, being hung & strung out
in South Africa.

Happy negro.   The news betrays your
joyous finger pop.   (The white man ain't
done wit your ass yet.)   The radio
reveals honkies' consistent cruelty
& america's indifference to lost
black blood.   In Soweto, 32 killed,
twenty something wounded, in Sharpsville
69 black pacifists made the streets red.
The media conjures a hurting

that never touched my body
I grow out raged dread locks,
feed my babies greens,
sing 'em old blues & gospel,
I grow dread full black rage,
a tradition make me wish
for prison or guns but
america sweet assimilate,
off-white black culture
gotta make it soft
for whitie to comprehend
this evil possessing me,
gotta rise above
their stink like a saint,
be a Tutu, be a King,
anti apart hate
and spit out
an american black poem:
anti apart
hate
art.

COUNTRY ETHICS & DONNA

When I lived in the country, I was friends with this white
girl who was real round & real dirty.   Like her hair was
kinda greasy & she didn't wear shoes & the edges of her
feet were dark & thick.   And she wore long greasy skirts,
spattered from the soup kitchen where she sometimes worked.

And she talked about this trip she was gonna take with her
old man, going off to his mountain or sumthin'.
And I said
'Well, how long you been with him?'
& she said
'Two weeks.'
And then she talked about her ex-old man.
And then she talked about the guy she was getting ready to
leave her new old man for.

One day I made two lasagna casseroles & chocolate chip cookies
for people who had been kind to me: some musicians who played
latin jazz & got me loaded on red hair humboldt home grown.
And Janet who bakes bread & is a christian.   And Donna who gave
me a feather roach clip when she found out I like to get high.
I was gonna give all nice people cookies, celebrating my food
stamps I got in the mail.

Food stamps was one of the hippest things about Humboldt county.
It only takes fifteen minutes to sign up, & they put them in the
mail, so you get them the next day, & you don't have to go
traipsing all across town, trying to cash them, looking at hard
faced people looking at you like you ain't got no sense just
'cause you ain't got no money.   Humboldt county puts they food
stamps in the mail, so you can go straight from the mail box
to the grocery store.

Most folks were poor there, the students & the working people.
The bums were poor too but that meant not eating in restaurants
& not having savings.   Most folks was warm, everybody was well
fed, & mostly everybody was happy.

I was so happy I took my food stamps presents, wrote out a note
that said:
Donna,
whatever you do, you cool wit me.
And left it with cookies & casseroles.

Then one time me & her was soppin' in the country rain, gettin'
very loaded, tryin' to decipher The Grand Sadness That's Always
With Us, & she said
'Ya know, ya gotta have faith, & read the signs,
like that time you brung me that casserole,
I had wished for a sign I wasn't gonna go hungry,
& Tom had just run off on me, & you brung me that casserole.
I knew it was a sign.'

I saw her one more time & she had a blond unshaven man in dark
boots & thick jacket.   She took me in the kitchen   tole me this
was her new boyfriend & she was goin' off to his mountain with
him & she loved him very much.   I tole her 'Alright,' gave her
my last five dollar food stamp & got on.

Then steady money started coming in, ya know, I must have been
working, or not spending money or had a good boyfriend, or some
sumthin', 'cause money kept coming in & I decided that to tithe
would be an excellent thing to do, so I send a check to her
address.   The letter was returned to me.   No such place, no
such mountain, they tole me.   And I have not heard from her
since.

LEAVING JANET

She baked bread.   Hanging in my mind is the odor of warm raisin
bread, baking.   She had thick arms, paste colored, and long,
not-thick brown hair, always clean & always braided.   She baked,
once a week she baked: hand-picked berry pie, french vanilla cookies,
and she cooked too, fried chicken & eggplant parmesan,
I could go into a trance over the food she fed me.

She talked of her husband Jim, who was albino-looking and skinny.
She told me stories with the moral being: And that's how he tricked
me into marrying him.   Stories that had stuff like: 'N seeing as
he tricked me into marrying him, well naturally, takin' into account
the fact I got tricked into it, well, the way I see it is, Yep,
good ole Janet was not into that man.

She was a christian.   She kept her hands crossed, but never her fingers.
She said to me, "All the ex-junkies in town go to our church.
You should go sometime.   You'd like it."

She grew pink budding flowers, 'n white ones, 'n blue ones.
Her fingers traced hummingbird patterns for me in the sky.
She grew vegetables from a place that was not distinguishable
as a garden, but vegetables came out of it nonetheless,
'n they were sweet, 'n we ate them.   The house was always dirty,
so dirty that friends said "How can you live like this?"
Once a week picked flowers, daffodils, magnolias,
'n spread them, thick as honey, everywhere in the house.

It was all her idea.

But then, the green on the way down the path home
darkened 'n thickened over my head, I dreamt of flying,
no evening walk was long or cool enough,
the bottoms of my feet began to itch,
'n all that, all together, happening at the same time
said Go.

Janet helped me pack.   Janet brought me string, 'n boxes, 'n showed me
how to fix my plants so they would not spill on the road.
Janet baked me cookies, 'n put them in a bag marked
'Good Luck Michelle.'   Good ole Janet.
She sure would be fun if she got loaded.
That good ole Janet, always a helping hand, always a hot meal,
'n it was true, 'n I ate my cookies
'n left.

SPIRITUAL WOMEN'S RESISTANCE

for Carolyn Fershtman

The sisters of my coven do mushrooms
right after magenta robes are hung.
We oil our breasts, the circle of witches
& priestess, nude, ready
to prepare pray & perform
ritual to receive the spells,
the triple hex, to trip the toes of men
on an evil walk, the zap for brutal police
& a start for the women's army
to combat rape.

On the quarter moon we meditate
on Venus's rise
to channel a knowing
back into our hands,
we must steady
tomorrow, we gather to gather
healing lights
charged
with a dead
serious
plan to fight.

GOD PROMISED US WATER THAT WAS WET

In the Eureka zoo, there is an ocelot who lives in a box about the size of a working class living room, who sits on a papier-mache tree, with no branches or leaves, just a trunk. Her fingers clutch the trunk of the papier-mache tree, & she stares out at the people who live in the city, all the pasty faced families & children with sticky hands, holding balloons, all the mothers & fathers who just let their children out of Sunday school, point & say, look, johnny, there is a wild animal. Look see. The ocelot's living room is painted with sky on the ceiling, clouds & puffs of plastic blue. On the floor someone painted a babbling brook, with stones & water, using the same color blue as the sky. On the three walls are painted trees, the same color as the papier-mache trunk & plants without flowers & more flat sky.

The ocelot's fingers clutch the trunk, but there is no other visible tension in her body. Her eyes are dazed & open towards the crowd. She does not blink or respond to the peanuts that are thrown at her. This bores the children, who run on to see cages of captured birds.

I laughed out loud when I first saw her, "That cat must feel like she's on acid or something. Look at her. Staring at the walls like that, thinking that this is life." I stared at her a long time, watching my thoughts, until there were no thoughts but streams of tears on my face. And sounds came, & the children began to stare at me harder than they were staring at the cat, & I was sobbing then, for all, for everything, for the three dimensions they made into two for cats, so Sunday afternoon will not be boring. And for me, alive in the cat, with three dimensions around me that made me sense a fourth, & how love is not thick enough, water not wet enough, children too old, too callous, too quickly.

They carried me out of the zoo that day. I missed certification by the skin of my teeth.

BOMBS AWAY /
Poem for the Church in Ocean Park

Once it was a place in time
way 'fore our thinkin' got rancid
w/ machine lust & logic
& logic got big on no heart & materialism
when regular folks could worked
these problems out
(by race mixing)
& the miracle of children born w/ out bitterness

but we done soured the home land
& our bright ocean:

when I go for a dip of calm
nature's water, my skin come out
skummy, a rash on my ass get me to
itchin' & thinkin' 'bout them
hard war-infested men
who didn't feel our planet's vulnerability
& like hot polished metal
better than clean beaches & peace.

So when the fizzle come,
when the final red burns
a slow mass suffer,
I want those military men & their women
to eat the toxic waste, get enough
sizzlin' in their pores
to bottom the fuck out

like pain could crack 'em up & out
of evil into nicety,
as if hurt could make a bad person good,
as if right wingers could say uncle
& make it alright, say, hey, I take it
all back, I been mean, I'm sorry,
I been greedy, I could be nice

now, let's build a nice world,
black & blue, pussy & dicks together.

And the hands of racially mixed
unborn children would be held
in a ritual by our mother
our water the sea
& send a hope back into the past,
our dirtied & anger filled now,
to greet & warm & lift us.

Michèlle T. Clinton is a poet / performance artist living in Los Angeles. She is a director of the Beyond Baroque poetry workshop. She has read & published extensively throughout Southern California. She is a featured artist on two Freeways Records spoken-words compilations, *English As A Second Language* & *Neighborhood Rhythms*, & is awaiting the release of an album of her work. She is a 1985 Alice Jackson Poetry Award winner.

This is her first volume of poetry.